Days That Changed The World

THE FIRST
MAN IN SPACE

David Cullen

WORLD ALMANAC® LIBRARY

Please visit our web site at: www.worldalmanaclibrary.com
For a free color catalog describing World Almanac® Library's
list of high-quality books and multimedia programs,
call 1-800-848-2928 (USA) or 1-800-387-3178 (Canada).
World Almanac® Library's fax: (414) 332-3567.

Library of Congress Cataloging-in-Publication Data

Cullen, David.
 The first man in space / by David Cullen.
   p. cm. — (Days that changed the world)
 Summary: Describes the 1961 flight of Soviet astronaut Yuri Gagarin, the first man in space,
as well as the scientific background to that flight and space exploration since then.
 Includes bibliographical references and index.
 ISBN 0-8368-5570-1 (lib. bdg.)
 ISBN 0-8368-5577-9 (softcover)
 1. Gagarin, Yuri Alekseyevich, 1934-1968—Juvenile literature. 2. Astronauts—Soviet Union—
Biography—Juvenile literature. [1. Gagarin, Yuri Alekseyevich, 1934-1968. 2. Astronauts.
3. Outer space—Exploration.] I. Title. II. Series.
TL789.85.G3C85   2004
629.45'0092—dc22
 [B]   2003060558

This North American edition first published in 2004 by
World Almanac® Library
330 West Olive Street, Suite 100
Milwaukee, WI 53212 USA

This U.S. edition copyright © 2004 by World Almanac® Library. Original edition copyright © 2003 by ticktock
Entertainment Ltd. First published in Great Britain in 2003 by ticktock Media Ltd., Unit 2, Orchard Business
Centre, North Farm Road, Tunbridge Wells, Kent TN2 3XF. Additional end matter copyright © 2004 by
World Almanac® Library.

We would like to thank: Tall Tree Ltd, Lizzy Bacon, and Ed Simkins for their assistance.

World Almanac® Library editor: Carol Ryback
World Almanac® Library cover design: Steve Schraenkler

Photo Credits:
t=top, b=bottom, c=center, l=left, r=right, OFC=outside front cover
Alamy: 12-13c, 34-35, 43c. CORBIS: 8, 9, 10, 11, 12l, 18, 20t, 39, 42b. Hulton Archive: 28.
NASA: 1, 6-7c, 7, 14-15, 15, 18-19, 22t, 30-31, 32, 33, 34, 35t, 36, 37, 38, 40, 43c, 43r.
Science Photo Library: 6, 14, 22t, 25, 26, 27.

Printed in Hong Kong

1 2 3 4 5 6 7 8 9 08 07 06 05 04

CONTENTS

*O*n April 12, 1961, Soviet Cosmonaut Yuri Gagarin became the first person to travel into space beyond Earth's atmosphere. His flight lasted a mere 108 minutes — but it marked the beginning of human exploration of the Universe. Before Gagarin's mission, the only living creatures that flew into space and returned alive were animals such as dogs, mice, and chimpanzees. Gagarin proved that humans were ready for that hazardous step beyond the safety of the atmosphere into a new frontier.

British forces fired Congreve rockets against Fort McHenry in Baltimore, Maryland, during the War of 1812. The ferocious rocket attack, which occurred in 1814, inspired attorney Francis Scott Key to write a poem — including the lines, "the rockets' red glare, the bombs bursting in air" — that became part of the lyrics of the U.S. national anthem.

Early experimentation with rockets dates back about one thousand years. In 1232, the Chinese developed gunpowder rockets. By the sixteenth century, Chinese official Wan-Hu recognized the potential for using rockets to transport people. According to legend, Wan-Hu strapped forty-seven rockets to a chair to create a flying machine.

Wan-Hu's failed attempt resulted in his death and the complete destruction of the chair.

For the next three hundred years, rockets were weapons of war rather than tools of exploration.

 the 1700s,
 dian leader
 yder Ali
 veloped
 ckets with
 etal cases
  fire at British
 vasion forces.
 li's son, Tippu
 ltan, also used metal
 ckets against the British
  the battles of Seringapatam
 1792

Robert Goddard developed the first liquid-fueled rocket in Auburn, Massachusetts. During its short (2.5-second) test flight, the rocket traveled 184 feet (56 meters) at 60 miles per hour (96.5 kilometers per hour) at an altitude of 41 feet (12.5 m).

and again in 1799. Afterwards, the British developed their own rocket-powered weapons. William Congreve's rocket design improved the accuracy of its flight path. The British fired Congreve rockets against the United States during the War of 1812.

Rocket technology really took off in the twentieth century. A huge advance came when scientists determined that liquid — rather than powdered — rocket fuels were necessary to produce enough power to travel into space.

The notion of space travel sparked imaginations and inspired hundreds of books, including Jules Verne's classic masterpiece, Voyages Extraordinaires, a collection of stories about extraordinary journeys.

JULES VERNE

DE LA TERRE A LA LUNE
autour de la Lune

VOYAGES EXTRAORDINAIRES
Collection Hetzel

Early experiments with space travel included sending a variety of animals, including chimpanzees, into space.

INTRODUCTION

Support towers break away as Vostok 1 propels Yuri Gagarin on his landmark voyage into space. The flight marked the beginning of human space travel and intensified the fierce race for technological superiority in space between the United States and the Soviet Union.

During Hitler's reign in Germany before and during World War II, Nazi scientists began developing rockets for use as long-distance missiles. Their experiments resulted in the V-2 (Vengeance Weapon 2 a long-range rocket that devastated several European cities. Although deadly, the V-2 rockets appeared too late to make a difference in the outcome of the war. After Germany's defeat, scientists behind the V-2 arrived in the United States or the Soviet Union and shared their secrets with the two superpowers. Their knowledge helped usher in a bold new age of space exploration.

On March 16, 1926, Robert Goddard succeeded in launching the world's first liquid-fueled rocket. The new fuels marked a significant step toward the conquest of space, a conquest intensified by developments during World War II.

In the late 1950s, the Soviet Union launched several Sputnik probes into space. And so began the frantic race between the oviets and the United States to be the first to send a man into space. Vostok, the first manned Soviet program, launched cosmonaut Yuri Gagarin into history. While the Soviets won that part of the space race, just over eight years later, the United States dwarfed the Soviet's achievement by landing a man on the Moon.

Today, we almost take space flight for granted. The United States and the Soviet Union shared many missions and much technology. Future space plans may include establishing a colony on the Moon, or traveling to Mars — or beyond. Whatever lies in the future, however, Gagarin's place in history as the first man to enter space is assured.

Today, space flights and space walks are almost routine duties for astronauts and cosmonauts. More than four hundred men and women have flown in space since Yuri Gagarin's historic mission.

Yuri Gagarin's amazing feat sparked off a wave of U.S. space missions. Astronaut John Glenn (left) holds two U.S. space records. He was the first American to orbit Earth in 1962. Glenn returned to space in 1998 aboard STS-95, the Space Shuttle Discovery, at the age of 77!

In the fall of 1944, during the last year of World War II, the Nazi unleashed a terrifying new weapon on Allied forces and civilians. The V-2 rocket was the second of the so-called German "vengeance" weapons. While the V-1 ("doodlebug") weapon was a slow-moving, jet-propelled flying bomb with a distinctive incoming sound, the rocket-powered V-2 flew at speeds of up to 3,500 mph (5,600 kph) — faster than the speed of sound. It soared high into the atmosphere, giving Allied forces little chance of detecting or destroying it before it a target.

A captured V-2 rocket stands on its mobile launch platform. The portability of the V-2s made it difficult for Allied forces to detect and destroy these rockets before launching.

SECRET *bases*

V-2 rockets were developed at a secret base at Peenemünde, Germany. Production continued there until an Allied air raid by the Royal Air Force almost completely destroyed the base in 1943. Scientists and technicians then moved to another secret site at Nordhausen, Germany. Slaves labored under astonishingly harsh conditions to assemble the V-2 rockets.

V-2 power

Using the technology that Robert Goddard pioneered nearly twenty years earlier, the V-2 was the first practical example of a rocket powered by liquid fuel. Its pointed body contained two tanks, one for liquid ethyl alcohol and the other for liquid oxygen. When the two liquids were pumped into the combustion chamber, they mixed and ignited, creating a powerful blast of hot gases that pushed the rocket forward. In the mid-1930s, Wernher von Braun led the team of scientists and engineers developing these rockets. He and Major General Walter R. Dornberger championed the use of rockets in warfare. Although the Treaty of Versailles that ended World War I banned the country of Germany from producing most kinds of weapons or developing rockets, von Braun's team received funding from the German military. In 1937, his team moved a secret base at Peenemünde in northwestern German on the Baltic coast. This remote site proved an ideal location for testing rockets safely over the Baltic Sea.

Winged wonders

The weakness of the V-2 was its lack of range, which was about 200 miles (320 kilometers). As the war raged on, German forces lost territory to the Allies, and needed longer-range missiles to continue fighting. At war's end, Allied troops discovered German plans for developing a winged version of the V-2. Wings would have allowed the V-2 to glide through the upper atmosphere, skimming across the stratosphere. Such a development would have greatly increased the rocket's range, creating the first intercontinental missile — and a weapon capable of hitting targets across the Atlantic Ocean on the east coast of the United States.

Rocket scientists

Allied and Soviet forces converging on Germany hoped to capture the technology that created the V-2 rockets. Wernher von Braun and a number of scientists from his team decided to surrender to U.S. troops instead of the Soviets. They were brought to the United States during Operation Paperclip.

After arrival in the U.S., von Braun and other rocket scientists and engineers continued their research under guard at several different military installations. Further testing and launching of the many captured V-2 rockets took place at the White Sands Proving Grounds in New Mexico.

Military rockets

Seven years after the end of World War II, von Braun became head of the U.S. Army ballistic program. Under his guidance, the program developed a string of rockets, including the Redstone and Juno rockets as well as the Pershing missile. They also developed the Jupiter-C, which later became the rockets for launching intermediate-range ballistic missiles. A *Juno 1* carried the first U.S. probe, *Explorer 1*, into orbit. Essentially a modified Redstone rocket, Braun redesigned it to travel nearly 17,000 mph

> *"It will free man from the remaining chains, the chains of gravity which still tie him to this planet."*
>
> Wernher von Braun discusses the possibilities of rocket flight

A V-2 rocket made no sound before impact, so an attack by these weapons was particularly devastating and deadly.

(27,000 kph) — fast enough to put a small satellite into orbit. His changes included adding a cluster of booster rockets and a fourth fuel stage to a Redstone rocket.

Missed opportunity

In 1954, the secret Army-Navy Project Orbiter program led by von Braun was scrapped in favor of Project Vanguard, another artificial satellite program, for political reasons. Had von Braun been allowed to continue with Project Orbiter, chances are the U.S. would have launched the world's first satellite.

Soviet rockets

Toward the end of World War II, Soviet fighting forces concentrated on obtaining German rocket technology. As the Soviet ("Red") Army advanced through Eastern Europe, it stumbled upon many of the Germans' secret manufacturing plants for the weapons. The Soviets confiscated whatever they could find of the V-2 rocket. When the war ended, Red Army forces returned to the Soviet Union with several hundred German scientists and engineers, as well as much of the V-2 technology.

Increasing power

Over the next ten years, these scientists and technicians worked under the guidance of Sergei Korolev, chief constructor for the development of long-range ballistic missiles. They rebuilt several V-2 rockets. During this time, the joint Soviet and German team built and flew a range of rockets with increased power. These included the R-1 (a direct copy of the German V-2), the G-4 (which greatly improved the range of the V-2 and was a prototype for the N-1 rocket — the Soviet attempt to send people to the Moon), and the R-5M (the first Soviet missile armed with a nuclear warhead). Finally, the team designed the R-7 rocket, the world's first intercontinental ballistic missile. Initially intended as a weapon of war, the R-7 could also function as a launch vehicle for space missions. By modifying the basic rocket design, Korolev and his technicians added several powerful rocket boosters and some

Wernher von Braun (below right) oversees the launch of a Saturn V rocket.

WERNHER *von Braun*

Wernher von Braun was born in Wirsitz, Germany, on March 23, 1912. He was obsessed with the possibility of space flight from an early age, and in 1925 he read a copy of *Die Rakete zu den Planetenräumen* ("The rocket in interplanetary space") by another rocket pioneer, Hermann Oberth. In this book, Oberth explained how a rocket could achieve enough speed to escape Earth's gravitational pull.

In 1930, Braun enrolled in the German Society for Space Travel, where he joined Oberth and helped him do tests on rocket motors.

After World War II, Braun was brought to the United States, where he oversaw the development of the U.S. space program. He developed the powerful Saturn V rockets that carried the Apollo capsules into space and on to the Moon. Wernher von Braun died of cancer in June, 1977.

SERGEI *Korolev*

Sergei Korolev was the pioneer behind the Soviet space program. Born in 1906, he became a cofounder of the Group for the Investigation of Reactive Motion (GIRD), based in Moscow. By the early 1930s, he and his colleagues were testing rocket-powered gliders, but after two years, the Soviet military asked them to develop a series of rocket-propelled missiles and aircraft. Korolev developed the RP-318, Russia's first rocket-propelled aircraft, but before the plane could fly, he was imprisoned at the height of Stalin's purges in 1937–1938. During his incarceration, Korolev spent time in transit on the Trans-Siberian Railway as well as a year working in the Kolyma gold mines in Siberia. Korolev was saved from a life of slavery with the outbreak of World War II, when Stalin recognized the importance of aeronautic engineers for the armed forces. After the war, Korolev developed the R-7 rocket, the world's first intercontinental ballistic missile. The R-7 carried the world's first space probe, *Sputnik 1*, into orbit. Korolev then developed the N-1 rocket program, the ultimate goal of which was to land Soviet cosmonauts on the Moon before U.S. astronauts arrived there. The United States is the only nation to land people on the Moon.

...ra rocket stages. Derivatives of the R-7 soon ...ame the workhorse for the Soviet space program ...the following fifty years. By 2000, R-7-type rockets ...completed over 1,628 launches with an almost ...ety-eight percent success rate. Both figures remain ...natched by any other production launch vehicle. ...R-7's heyday came on October 4, 1957, when it ...sted the first man-made object— a small probe ...ned *Sputnik 1* — into space.

...to space

...course of world history changed the day the Soviet ...on announced the successful launch of its orbiting ...ficial satellite. This pivotal event marked the start ...he space age and the beginning of the space race ...ween the world's two superpowers, the United States ...the Soviet Union. *Sputnik 1* itself was not ...plicated. It was a silver aluminum sphere about ...size of a basketball that sent back a simple radio ...al. Weighing in at 184 pounds (84 kilograms), ...as much heavier than the intended U.S. satellites, ...earliest of which weighed just 31 pounds (14 kg). ...weight difference made U.S. scientists realize that

the Soviet rockets were bigger and more powerful than those launched by the United States. *Sputnik 1* also prompted U.S. fears that if the Soviets could launch a probe into space, they posed a very real threat of launching missiles aimed at the United States from space. In response, in 1958, the U.S. boosted space funding and created the National Aeronautics and Space Administration (NASA).

Sergei Korolev headed the Soviet Union's space program. He died in 1966 as a result of a botched medical operation.

SPUTNIK *1*

Sputnik 1 was hurriedly put together in just a few months when it was discovered that the original probe was not going to be ready in time (this probe later became *Sputnik 3*). *Sputnik 1* was even built without preliminary drawings due to the limited time schedule. Inside the aluminum ball was the radio equipment, which was powered by three silver zinc batteries that provided one watt of power. Once in space, the probe completed an orbit once every 96 minutes. At its closest point, (perigee) it was 142 miles (228 km) above Earth's surface, while at its farthest point (apogee), it was 588 miles (946 km) above Earth. The probe remained in orbit until early 1958, when it fell back to Earth and burned up in the upper atmosphere.

1957

4 ОКТЯБРЯ
в Советском Союзе произведен.
запуск ПЕРВОГО искусственного
СПУТНИКА ЗЕМЛИ

3 НОЯБРЯ
в Советском Союзе произведен.
запуск ВТОРОГО искусственного
СПУТНИКА ЗЕМЛИ

A Soviet postcard celebrates the launches of the early Sputnik probes.

Rhesus monkeys are among several creatures that have also been used for test flights into space.

Another first

Less than a month after the launch of *Sputnik 1*, the Soviets shocked the U.S. again with the launch of *Sputnik 2*. This probe was far more sophisticated than its predecessor and it also carried the first living creature to travel into space, a small dog named "*Laika*" (Russian for "Barker"). Launched on November 3, 1957 on top of another modified R-7 rocket, this cone-shaped spacecraft had a compartment that was large enough for her to lie down, as well as sections containing radio equipment and scientific instruments. During the flight, Laika was supplied with food and water in a gelatinized form, as well as oxygen to breathe. She was fitted with a bag for collecting waste. A harness kept her secure.

nsors attached to Laika indicated that she
vived the high-gravity forces during blastoff
well as the weightlessness of space, although she
s a little agitated by the flight. Nevertheless, the
ta that came back from these instruments proved
invaluable starting point on the path to humans
veling in space. Sadly, there was no way of
urning the *Sputnik 2* capsule to Earth safely, so
ka's voyage was a one-way trip. Recent evidence
icates that the innocent animal most likely died
m heat exposure within hours of launching.

xplorer

utnik 1 and 2 shocked the United States into
elerating its space program. However, another
hree months passed before the United States
launched a space probe.

On January 31, 1958, *Explorer 1* blasted into space
atop a Jupiter-C rocket developed by Wernher von
Braun. Instruments aboard *Explorer 1* made an
important discovery. An experiment designed by
physicist James A. Van Allen revealed the presence
of intense belts of radiation, called the Van Allen
Radiation Belts, surrounding Earth over the equator.
Formed by Earth's magnetic field, these belts trap
some of the solar and cosmic particles before they
enter the lower atmosphere. So although it was
much smaller in size than its Soviet predecessors,
Explorer 1 highlighted the essential difference
between the two countries' space-race efforts.
While Soviet rockets were more powerful and
could lift heavier payloads, the U.S. led the way in
miniaturization, creating small scientific instruments
that could fit into more compact spacecraft that
required less-powerful rockets to lift them into orbit.

ANIMALS *in space*

Since Laika's extraterrestrial journey,
both the United States and the Soviet
Union launched a variety of animal
species into space. The Soviets used dogs
in their early flights to see how they
reacted to outer space. NASA sent
chimpanzees on Mercury test flights to
learn how they handled reentry into the
atmosphere and splashdown into the
ocean. Since then, the array of living
things sent into space includes simple
single-celled creatures such as amoeba, as
well as fish, birds, jellyfish, insects, frogs,
and mice. Scientists believe that by
studying how spaceflight affects these
animals, they will discover how to keep
human passengers healthy on long space
missions. Many people consider the use
of animal astronauts a form of animal
cruelty. In response to these concerns,
NASA appointed Joseph T. Bieliteki,
DVM, as its Chief Veterinary Officer
in 1996. Bieliteki established bioethical
principles for the treatment and
use of animals in NASA's space-life
science research.

*"Space travel is
bunk (nonsense)."*

**Sir Harold Spencer-Jones, the
United Kingdom's Astronomer
Royal, two weeks before
Sputnik 1's historic flight
in 1957**

*"Sputnik was one
of the finest things
Russia ever did
for us... It waked
this country up."*

**Vannevar Bush,
U.S. scientist, 1957**

Toward the end of the 1950s, the Soviet Union and the United States regularly sent spacecraft carrying animals and scientific experiments into space. Results from these early missions indicated that the next step — sending a human into space — was a realistic possibility. Both superpowers focused their attention on being the first to achieve this goal. They poured enormous amounts of money and manpower into their space programs. The race to send a human being into orbit began in earnest.

Sergei Korolev poses with one of the dogs trained for spaceflight. Korolev headed the Vostok program as well as Project Section 9.

MAR/1/57

Soviet scientists, under the guidance of Sergei Korolev, decided upon a suborbital (incomplete orbit) flight for the first manned mission. On March 1, 1957, Korolev established Project Section 9 to design the new spacecraft. In a little over a month, Project scientists devised plans to adapt the R-7 rocket for launching separate missions involving a manned spacecraft and an unmanned lunar probe.

NOV/1/57

U. S. aeronautical engineer Maxime Faget presented his concepts for manned spaceflights. Faget played a key role in designing the Mercury space capsule's heat shield and many of its other components.

After considering many designs, the Soviets opted for a spherical capsule attached to a small service module (center). Vostok's service module, designed to break away before reentry, contained batteries that supplied power and oxygen for life-support systems.

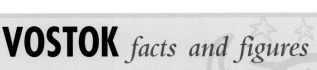

VOSTOK *facts and figures*

The one-person Vostok capsule measured 7.5 feet (2.3 m) across and weighed 5.2 tons (4.7 tonnes). Although a ground crew controlled the mission's flight, the cosmonaut could maneuver the craft in case of an emergency. Three small portholes allowed the rider a view of space. Vostok (which means "east" in Russian) could spend up to ten days in orbit.

AN/1/58

viet engineers began developing plans
the manned space probe. They considered
veral competing designs. A one-man spacecraft
s chosen as most appropriate for the mission.

APR/1/58

The spherical *Vostok* capsule was ready by April.
It would fly at an altitude of about 155 miles
(250 km). During reentry — and after dropping
to an altitude of about 6 miles (10 km) —
the pilot would eject, open a parachute,
and land separately from the capsule.
In order to claim the first
successful manned spaceflight,
the Soviets kept this fact
a closely guarded secret.

JUN/1/58

In early June 1958, designs
for the U.S. Mercury capsule were
also close to completion. Initial concepts
included a blunt-shaped capsule that used
parachutes to slow it down after reentry
and a winged spacecraft that would glide
to a landing at an airfield. Space engineers
settled on the blunt-shaped design for the
Mercury capsule.

> "We had absolute
> confidence in
> Comrade Korolev
> … you could see
> passion burning
> in his eyes …
> he had unlimited
> energy and
> determination."
>
> *Nikita Khrushchev, 1964*

The Mercury astronauts were
allowed to name their own capsules.
Alan Shepard named his Mercury
capsule Freedom 7.

MERCURY
facts and figures

Engineers designed the Mercury
capsule to spend up to 24 hours in
space. The roughly triangular, one-
person craft stood 11 feet (3.5 m) tall
and sloped to a base 6 feet (2 m)
across. Overall, it weighed
2,400 pounds (1,100 kg), of
which the heat shield alone
weighed 600 pounds (272 kg).

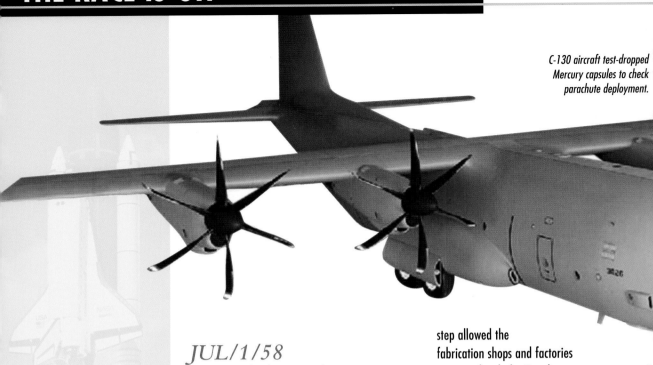

C-130 aircraft test-dropped Mercury capsules to check parachute deployment.

JUL/1/58

Designers and technicians in the Soviet space program decided to concentrate on planning a manned flight that would perform a complete Earth orbit. Korolev was confident that a modified R-7 launcher could carry a manned spacecraft into orbit. On July 1, 1958, Korolev met with members of the highest Soviet political body, the *Politburo*, to explain the advantages of manned spaceflight.

SEP/1/58

The Soviets created a department devoted to the development of a manned spacecraft. The first construction drawings of the Vostok capsule appeared on September 1, 1958. This important step allowed the fabrication shops and factories associated with the Vostok program to start testing the spacecraft's systems. These tests began only two weeks after the completion of the drawings. By the end of autumn 1958, the Council of Chief Designers approved the Vostok capsule and authorized Korolev to proceed with manned spaceflights at the earliest possible date. The Council also decided to adapt the Vostok design for a line of spy satellites called Zenit.

OCT/1/58

Meanwhile, U.S. technicians worked on developing what would become the Mercury capsules. Chief Designer Maxime Faget and his team invented a special couch designed to help the astronauts withstand the high-gravity forces of liftoff and reentry. Tests on full-scale capsules dropped from C-130 planes began on October 9, 1958. These tests checked the feasibility of using parachutes to safely slow down the spacecraft as it descended into the atmosphere. Further tests documented not only the descent, but also the retrieval of the capsules from the Atlantic Ocean.

R-7 *rocket*

The Soviet R-7 rocket was the world's first intercontinental ballistic missile (ICBM). It was 92 feet (28 m) long and 10 feet (3 m) in diameter, with a range of nearly 5,500 miles (8,800 km). Four strap-on boosters surrounding the base of the rocket acted as the first stage *(see page 22)*. The Soviets adapted the R-7 into a launch vehicle for Vostok and Soyuz space missions by adding another stage and a capsule. NATO (the North Atlantic Treaty Organization) labeled it the SS-7, or "Sapwood."

DEC/17/58

SA officially announced "Project Mercury"
the public on December 17, 1958.

APR/9/59

Further tests continued
on the Mercury capsules
during the winter of 1958
and spring of 1959. Attention
turned to pilots for the capsules.
On April 9, 1959, following
a rigorous program of
physical and mental tests,
NASA announced the
seven Mercury astronauts

who were selected from a field of 110 military
pilots. The seven men with the right stuff included
Alan B. Shepard Jr., John H. Glenn Jr.,
Virgil I. ("Gus") Grissom, L. Gordon Cooper,
Donald ("Deke") Slayton,
M. Scott Carpenter, and
Walter ("Wally") Schirra Jr.

MAR/1/60

Back in the Soviet Union,
the development of
the Vostok capsule
and the Zenit spy
satellite was not going
as smoothly as hoped.

*Although people think
of space as being a cold
place, the majority of
a space-suit's temperature
controls are dedicated to
keeping the person cool.*

SPACE *protection*

Astronauts and cosmonauts wear
special suits to protect them from
the harsh conditions when they
travel into space. A space suit
provides air pressure similar
to that found on Earth,
as well as oxygen to
breathe. Also, a space suit
helps regulate body
temperature
and protects
the person from
the high levels
of radiation
found in
space.

THE RACE IS ON

Soviet military officials became increasingly angry with Korolev. They felt he was devoting more of his time to the Vostok space project than to Zenit. In the meantime, pilot selection for the Vostok program began. On March 1, 1960, an elite group of twenty test pilots reported for duty. Financial considerations reduced the Soviet team to just six pilots. Among them, one pilot consistently received top grades from all the instructors. His name was Yuri Gagarin.

Yuri Gagarin loved to fly. After his first flight in a Yak-18 fighter, he said, "That first flight filled me with pride and gave meaning to my whole life."

DEC/19/60

In contrast to the Soviet program, Project Mercury progressed smoothly. By the end of 1960, NASA began testing unmanned Mercury capsules. After two failed attempts, NASA completed a successful launch in December 1960. Just over a month later, another successful mission launched a chimpanzee named Ham into space. The chimp was recovered in good physical condition after splashdown. When his handlers later showed him the spacecraft, however, Ham made it clear that he had no further interest in participating in the Mercury program!

YURI *Gagarin*

Yuri Gagarin was born near the town of Gzatsk, Russia, on March 9, 1934. He grew up on a collective (jointly-owned) farm, where his father worked as a carpenter. Gagarin attended a trade school near Moscow and graduated in 1951 as a molder. He then continued his studies in metalworking. While a student, Gagarin enrolled in flying lessons. His natural talent for flying quickly developed, so when he completed his college course, he entered the Soviet Air Force cadet school near Orenburg, Russia.

Gagarin graduated from flight school in 1957. It soon became evident that he was no ordinary flier. Gagarin became a test pilot, flying and testing the latest experimental aircraft. During this time, he learned about the fledgling Soviet space program and volunteered for training as a cosmonaut.

TRAINING *for space*

Astronaut training for a space shuttle mission begins with courses on aircraft safety and emergency procedures, ejection, parachuting, and wilderness survival. Pilots and mission specialists make test flights on high-performance T38 jets. Weightlessness training occurs inside specially converted planes or enormous water tanks. In 1996, the Neutral Buoyancy Lab (NBL) in Houston, Texas, opened for underwater training. The NBL measures 200 feet (61 m) long, 100 feet (30 m) wide, and 40 feet (12 m) deep. Inside, a full-scale mock-up of the shuttle payload bay and air lock allows astronauts to familiarize themselves with the layout in a simulated weightless environment. The final portion of the training occurs on the Shuttle Mission Simulator. The Simulator replicates different parts of a mission to produce virtual situations, such as blastoff, touchdown, or an emergency.

Left: Astronauts train for future space missions as they experience the effects of weightlessness inside a specially adapted plane. By dropping down very suddenly, the plane creates "free fall" — a weightless environment similar to that of a space mission. Free fall often causes nausea, so the astronauts refer to the plane by its nickname, the "Vomit Comet."

During its path around Earth, the probe reached a maximum altitude of 109 miles (175 km). As before, the mannequin ejected from the capsule and descended by parachute. Zvezdochka was recovered safely when the capsule landed. Over the next two weeks, final preparations continued for the historic first spaceflight by a human. On April 3, 1961, the Soviets issued a formal decree authorizing the first manned flight of the Vostok capsule.

MAR/9/61

...ce they resolved the arguments over the military ...d civilian nature of the Vostok space program, ...viet scientists progressed rapidly with the ...velopment of the capsule. On March 9, 1961, ...og named Chernushka flew in a capsule ...h a mannequin nicknamed Ivan Ivanovich. ...e mannequin (*"maket"* in Russian) was ejected ...m the capsule after reentry and Chernushka ...s recovered safely.

MAR/25/61

...e pace of the Soviet program accelerated. ... the end of March, they launched another test ...ht of a Vostok probe. This probe contained a dog ...ned Zvezdochka and the dummy Ivan Ivanovich.

APR/9/61

Six days later, the Soviets chose Yuri Gagarin as the first Vostok cosmonaut. Gagarin excelled at every stage of his training. He withstood enormous physical demands during training and survived a sensory-deprivation test where he spent 24 hours in a soundless, completely dark room. The Soviets officially announced Gagarin's selection two days later, on April 11, 1961 — the day before his historic flight.

"What is it that makes a man willing to sit on top of an enormous Roman candle... and wait for someone to light the fuse?"

Tom Wolfe, author of The Right Stuff (1979)

APRIL 12, 1961

At dawn on April 12, 1961, the Baikonur Cosmodrome buzzed with activity. Final launch preparations were underway for the shining rocket that stood bathed in floodlights. As the Sun rose, a doctor walked into a room and woke the person sleeping inside. Yuri Gagarin opened his eyes, got out of bed, calmly performed his morning exercise routine, and dressed as if it were an ordinary day. Then he walked into another room where doctors waited to perform a final check-up to ensure that Gagarin was fit for his historic fligh

Gagarin wore an orange space suit for the mission.

READY FOR ACTION

At six in the morning, Gagarin met with members of the State Commission who were overseeing the mission. The meeting was short; its purpose was to pronounce Gagarin and the *Vostok 1* ready for the flight. He donned some special light overalls over which he wore a bright orange space suit and helmet. The suits were designed to protect the cosmonaut in the event of a failure in the airtight seal of the spacecraft and to shield him from high radiation levels. Gagarin then proceeded to the rocket, meeting with the State Commission one last time to report that he was ready for the flight.

IN THE COCKPIT

08:00

In the final hour before launch, Gagarin was fastened into the specially designed seat. The hatch of the spacecraft was shut and sealed. Preparations continued outside, and — in order to keep him relaxed — a friendly banter took place between the cosmonaut and the control room. To help pass the time, music played over the intercom.

Gagarin in the seat of Vostok
He named his capsule "Swallo

"A fit comrade, never loses heart, a man of principles, bold and steadfast, modest and simple, decisive, a leader."

— Gagarin's character as summed up by his fellow cosmonauts

"He submits useful suggestions at meetings. Always sure of his resources... very difficult, if not impossible to upset... Stands out among his colleagues thanks to his great scope of active attention, bright mind and quick reaction."

— a summary of Gagarin's abilities by his instructors

"The stratosphere is not the limit for you!"

— a doctor's reaction to Gagarin's physical and mental strength

COUNTDOWN BEGINS   09:00

Before too long, however, the music died down and the camera inside the cabin was switched on. Inside the control room, Sergei Korolev picked up the microphone and said, "'Dawn' calling 'Cedar' (Gagarin's call sign). The countdown is about to start." "Roger. Feeling fine," Gagarin replied. "Excellent spirits, ready to go." As the seconds ticked by, the final phases of the preparation were carried out. "Switch to 'go' position," came the command. "Idle run." The fueling tower moved smoothly away from the side of the rocket. With a tremendous roar, the rockets fired up and the jib carrying the power cables swung away.

After the last ch the countdown bega and at 9:07 A.M., Vostok shot out of the launch pad.

LIFT-OFF

`09:0`

As the powerful motors beneath Gagarin's spacecraft ignited, the supporting arms around the rock fell away like the petals of a flow The enormous rocket then lifted clear of the launchpad and rose into the air. Gagarin jubilantly shouted "*Poyekhali*" ("Off we g Gagarin felt calm and displayed his usual precise and methodical manner. The only weird sensation he reported occurred when Serge Korolev's voice broke through over the radio to tell him that seventy seconds had elapsed. "Can it really be only seventy?" he said. "What long seconds!"

Vostok 1's boosters power the rocket into space.

INTO SPACE

`09:22`

The R-7 rocket, like any other space launch vehicle, worked on the principle of using stages. As a rocket climbs through the air, it uses a large amount of fuel. This means that before too long, the rocket is left with a lot of "dead" weight, in the form of empty fuel and oxidizer tanks as we as the support structures that hold them. To relieve the rocket of this dead weight, the empty tanks and supports are jettisoned, leaving the rocket much lighter. The rocket motors of t next stage then fire up to push the now-lighter rocket higher into the atmosphere. Som rockets, such as the powerful Saturn V that sent *Apollo 11* to the Moon, used three stages to push them faster and farther. During the first fifteen minutes of Gagarin's flight, the powerful rocket motors of the R-7 blazed away, pushing the *Vostok 1* capsule higher into space. First, the strap-on boosters on the side of the rocket burned out and fell away, followed shortly by the powerful motors of the first stage. At 09:22 A.M., rocket motors on the final stage burned out. Gagarin starte to experience the first effects of the weightless environment of space. Anything not fastened down, including notepads and pens, started floating around the cab As Gagarin looked out of the portholes on his capsule, he saw a sight that no oth human ever witnessed before — the blue globe of Earth from space.

Earth, the blue planet, seen from space.

VIEWPOINT

"I say 'until we meet again' to you, dear friends, as we always say to each other when setting off on a long journey. How I should like to embrace you all — my friends and those with whom I am not acquainted, strangers and the people nearest and dearest to me!"

— Gagarin in a pre-flight interview

"In a few minutes a mighty ship will carry me aloft to distant space. What can I say to you in these last moments before launch? At this instant the whole of my life seems to be condensed into one wonderful moment. To be the first to enter the cosmos, to engage, single-handed, in an unprecedented duel with nature — could one dream of anything more?"

— Gagarin before the launch

"Am I happy to be setting off on a cosmic flight? Of course. In all ages and epochs people have experienced the greatest happiness before they start upon new voyages of discovery."

— Gagarin in a pre-flight interview

INTO ORBIT `09:32`

Ten nail-biting minutes passed before data relayed from the *Vostok 1* capsule confirmed that it succeeded in attaining a safe orbit. For the next 89 minutes, Gagarin sailed around the world at altitudes varying from 105 miles (169 km) to 196 miles (315 km). During the flight, he had no direct control over the capsule. However, a key kept in an envelope in the cabin allowed him to override the automatic systems in an emergency. After just one orbit of Earth, the retro-rockets on the bottom of the spacecraft fired to slow the capsule down. Gagarin began his descent back into the atmosphere.

The capsule of Vostok 1 begins its descent back to Earth.

Gagarin in the capsule on the way back to Earth.

REENTRY `10:51`

Not everything went smoothly for Gagarin as his capsule started to descend. A small service module that supplied power and oxygen was designed to break away before reentry, but it snagged on a bundle of wire and remained connected to the main capsule. The extra module caused Gagarin's capsule to buck and spin wildly as it reentered Earth's atmosphere. Fortunately, searing temperatures outside burned away the wire bundle, separating the service module and allowing Gagarin's capsule to assume the correct reentry position.

APRIL 12, 1961

VIEWPOINT

"On...12 April 1961, the Soviet spaceship Vostok was put in orbit around the Earth with me on board... there was a good view of the Earth which had a distinct and pretty blue halo. It had a smooth transition from pale blue, blue, dark blue, violet and absolutely black. It was a magnificent picture."

— Yuri Gagarin in his official statement after the flight

"Yuri personified the eternal youth of our people. He combined within himself, in a most happy blend, the attributes of courage, an analytical mind, and exceptional industry."

— Sergei Korolev describing Yuri Gagarin's character

"What pleased us about Gagarin was that in 108 minutes he was able to see a great deal and enrich science with valuable information and conclusions."

— Sergei Korolev explaining Gagarin's importance to the mission

EJECTION   `10:53`

With flames licking the outside of the spherical capsule, *Vostok 1* continued its descent into the atmosphere. Once inside the atmosphere, the flames stopped, but the capsule continued to fall rapidly. Soviet scientists determined that a cosmonaut would not survive the impact of the fall inside the capsule. Gagarin ejected from the capsule at an altitude of about 5 miles (7 km) and parachuted safely to Earth's surface.

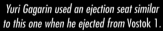
Yuri Gagarin used an ejection seat similar to this one when he ejected from Vostok 1.

DOWN TO EARTH   `10:54`

Meanwhile, the *Vostok 1* capsule deployed its own parachutes to slow it down. Cosmonauts on all other Vostok missions also ejected from their capsules, but cosmonauts for different missions stayed within their capsules until touchdown. All U.S. astronauts stayed inside their capsules which — until the advent of the Space Shuttle — always splashed down in the ocean.

Gagarin and his Vostok 1 capsule parachuted down separately over land.

THE LANDING 10:55

Gagarin landed at 10:55 A.M.
His entire mission lasted only
108 minutes, but it had made history.
Who met the hero after his monumental
mission? A confused old woman, her
granddaughter — and their cow!
However, a crowd of farm workers
quickly gathered around the cosmonaut.
They learned about the mission over
the radio and rushed to the scene
to greet the cosmonaut on his return.
Nearby, *Vostok 1*'s scorched capsule
lay in a neighboring field.

SECRETS & SUCCESS 11:05

Ten minutes after Gagarin's landing, a helicopter
appeared over the horizon to recover the
cosmonaut and his capsule. News of the success
spread rapidly around the world as television,
radio, newspapers, and magazines picked up
the story. However, Soviet authorities omitted
any mention of Gagarin's ejection and
parachute-assisted descent from the official
news release. According to rules set by
the FAI (La Fédération Aéronautique
Internationale) — the organization that
governs all air and space records —
any person or persons riding into space
must remain inside the capsule until it
touched down. If the FAI had learned
the truth about Gagarin's descent, it may have
disqualified his flight! Back at the Cosmodrome,
Gagarin met with one of Moscow's leading
politicians before going to meet the
team of technicians who helped put
him into space. Sergei Korolev,
their leader, was the first to
greet and congratulate him.

Newsweek

THE VOYAGE OF Yuri Gagarin
—SPECIAL SECTION—

Gagarin's achievement made headlines
around the world.

*Vostok 1's scorched remains landed
in a Soviet field.*

Two days after his historic trip, Gagarin traveled to the Soviet capital to meet the public. He boarded a special plane at Saratov and took off for Moscow. About 31 miles (50 km) short of the city, a flight of Soviet fighter jets swooped in to escort the hero on the last leg of his journey.

> *"I could have gone on flying through space forever."*
>
> Yuri Gagarin, quoted in
> The New York Times,
> April 14, 1961

Welcoming committee

As the plane taxied to a halt outside the Vnukovo Airport Terminal in Moscow, a red carpet unrolled to welcome Gagarin. At the other end, a group of Communist Party officials and government leaders waited to greet the cosmonaut. Gagarin delivered a short speech reporting the successful mission to the adoring crowd. He then turned to receive the congratulations of the assembled politicians, and welcomed his wife, Valentina, his children, and his parents. The entire group then rode in a cortége of cars to take them on the journey to Red Square for the official welcoming ceremony.

Human corridor

Along the 18-mile (30-km) route from the airport, Gagarin saw crowds everywhere shouting his name, waving flags and banners, and throwing flowers. At Red Square, a huge crowd in the square — and an even larger audience watching the event on televisions all over Europe — waited to hear his speech. In it, Gagarin thanked the Communist Party and the Soviet government, as well as the scientists, technicians, engineers, and workers who made his mission possible. He also declared that he and his fellow cosmonauts were prepared to travel farther out into space to explore the expanses of the Universe.

Thousands of people thronged into Red Square in the heart of Moscow to see their new hero.

SOVIET *honors*

That night, Gagarin became the first of eleven cosmonauts from 1961 though 1965 who received the Soviet Union's two highest honors. The Order of Lenin recognized Gagarin's outstanding services to the revolutionary movement and to the Soviet State and society. The Gold Star of Hero of the Soviet Union acknowledged services to the State that involved unusually heroic behavior.

Gagarin proudly wears the decorations he received for his historic flight.

Evening reception

at evening, in honor of the first manned space ght, Gagarin and his family attended an evening ception in the Grand Kremlin Palace in Moscow. ring the event, Leonid Brezhnev, chairman the Presidium of the Supreme Soviet, presented garin with the Order of Lenin and the Gold Star Hero of the Soviet Union — two of the Soviet ion's highest awards.

A new life

garin's life changed completely after his flight. was bombarded with requests for press nferences, radio and television interviews, and her public appearances. Throughout them all, garin remained determined to continue his rmal duties and training. This determination came apparent in one interview when a urnalist asked him whether he'd be able to rest his laurels for the remainder of his life. "Rest?" responded. "In the Soviet Union everybody rks, and those who work the hardest of all e the best-known people, the heroes of the Soviet ion and heroes of Socialist labor, of whom there thousands in the country." Gagarin returned Star City, where he became an instructor to his low cosmonauts, preparing them for future space ssions. However, despite his hectic new life, garin found time to relax. He enjoyed spending e with his family, and loved water skiing, ning, and hunting in the woods around his home.

He also discovered a new pastime in writing and often wrote well into the night. By the time of his death in 1968, Gagarin had written two books, *The Way to the Cosmos*, and *Psychology and Space*, which he coauthored with Vladimir Lebedev.

STAR *City*

Situated east of Moscow, Star City was built in 1960 with the sole purpose of training cosmonauts for space missions. It contained all the facilities of a town, including shops, leisure facilities, a school, and a hospital. Star City is still an active space-training facility for Soviet cosmonauts as well as foreign astronauts.

Statesman

Countries around the world invited the cosmonaut to visit them on goodwill missions, and Gagarin undertook many of these in the years after his spaceflight. During this time, he visited communist countries such as Bulgaria, Czechoslovakia, Hungary, and Poland, as well as Western nations, including Great Britain, Canada, and Norway. Gagarin discovered himself increasingly in demand back in his home country. His obligations became more formal after his election as a deputy for the Supreme Soviet of the USSR *(see Supreme Soviet box, page 29)* for the Smolensk region.

Vostok

The Soviets continued the Vostok program. Less than four months after the launch of *Vostok 1*, Gherman Titov blasted into space inside *Vostok 2*. This time, the cosmonaut spent an entire day in space and completed seventeen Earth orbits before reentry. During the flight, Titov took control of the capsule but suffered from space sickness. As with Gagarin's mission, problems with the separation of the service module from the reentry capsule occurred. As soon as the wires holding the service module burned away, everything went fine. Once again, the cosmonaut ejected from the capsule before it touched down.

Gagarin received warm greetings in every country he visited. The United Kingdom's prime minister, Harold Macmillan, was among the heads of state who welcomed Gagarin.

Joint mission

The next Vostok mission marked another fir in space. This time, two Vostok capsules launched within a day of each other in the first joint space mission. *Vostok 3*, containing cosmonaut Adrian Nikolayev, launched on August 11, 1962, while *Vostok 4*, carrying cosmonaut Pavel Popovich, launched the following day. During this mission, the two spacecraft passed within 3 miles (5 km) of each other. Popovich's mission was cut short, however. Durin his preflight briefing, he had been told to say tha he was "observing storm

Thirty-four-year-old Yuri Gagarin died on March 27, 1968 during a test flight of a MiG-15 fighter jet like the one pictured here.

...e experienced the
...ne space sickness
...ov felt on the *Vostok 2*
...ssion. Ground Control
...uld then bring him
...ck down. Unfortunately,
...povich really did see thunderstorms in the
...lf of Mexico and reported this to Ground Control.
...e technicians misunderstood, and — believing
...t he was ill — brought him back early.

First woman in space

...e next Vostok mission was another joint one,
...h *Vostok 5* and *Vostok 6* again launched within
...ay of each other. This time, however, one
...the spacecraft carried the first woman into
...ce. Valentina Tereshkova blasted into orbit
...ide *Vostok 6* on June 16, 1963. Like the
...vious Vostok mission, the two probes passed
...hin 3 miles (5 km) of each other and also
...ablished radio communication between the
... orbiting cosmonauts.

Tragic end

All this time, Gagarin worked hard to complete his training at the Soviet Air Academy. He eventually finished his course there and qualified with distinction as an engineer. His real passion was to travel into space again, and Gagarin continued with his cosmonaut training with that goal in mind. "Being a cosmonaut is my profession," he said, "and I did not choose it just to make the first flight and then give it up." Sadly, Gagarin never traveled in space again. He died on March 27, 1968, when his MiG-15 fighter jet crashed during a routine training mission near Moscow.

SUPREME *Soviet*

Yuri Gagarin was a deputy in the Supreme Soviet, the highest legislative body in the Soviet Union. The general population elected the members of the Supreme Soviet assembly — which met twice yearly or during emergencies — but in reality, the assembly wielded limited powers. It acted more or less as a rubber stamp for the Politburo and the Communist Party.

The right stuff

The Soviets beat the U.S. into space by less than one month. Unfortunately, Alan Shepard's mission for a March 24, 1961 flight was postponed until further tests on some missile modifications were tested. Otherwise, Shepard would have beaten Gagarin into space by more than two weeks! Instead, on May 5, 1961, Shepard blasted into space inside a Mercury capsule. His flight only lasted fifteen minutes and he did not orbit Earth.

Shepard's *Freedom 7* capsule reached an altitude of 116 miles (186 km), before reentering the atmosphere and landing in the Atlantic Ocean.

More missions

The second Mercury mission, with astronaut "Gus" Grissom aboard the *Liberty Bell 7*, blasted off on July 21, 1961. Grissom's suborbital flight reached an altitude of 118 miles (190 km). After splashdown, he nearly drowned when the capsule's hatch blew open prematurely. Following Grissom's flight, Soviet cosmonaut Gherman Titov made the second Vostok flight, this time spending an entire day in orbit. Titov's achievement changed U.S. plans to send all seven Mercury astronauts on short, suborbital flights. NASA scrapped further suborbital flights and planned for an Earth orbit. The agency substituted a more powerful Atlas rocket for the Redstone rocket used on previous Mercury flights. On February 20, 1962, John Glenn orbited Earth in *Friendship 7* during a mission that lasted 4 hours and 55 minutes. Glenn took control of the capsule when one of the automatic systems failed, but this did not affect the overall success of the mission. He landed in the Atlantic Ocean southeast of the Bahamian archipelago, near Grand Turk Island, part of the Turks and Caicos Islands.

The seven Mercury astronauts were (back row, left to right), Alan B. Shepard Jr., Virgil I. ("Gus") Grissom, and L. Gordon Cooper; (front row, left to right), Walter ("Wally") Schirra, Donald ("Deke") Slayton, John H. Glenn Jr., and M. Scott Carpenter.

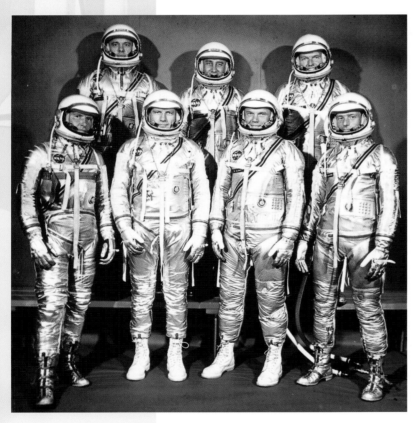

CAPE *Canaveral*

In 1949, Cape Canaveral, Florida, replaced the missile testing station at White Sands, New Mexico. Initially established as a missile testing base, Cape Canaveral hosted the launches of the earliest space missions, including *Explorer 1* and the Mercury missions. In 1963, NASA acquired land on Merritt Island next to Cape Canaveral from which to launch the larger rockets required for the proposed Apollo lunar missions. After Kennedy's assassination in 1963, NASA's entire complex was renamed the John F. Kennedy Space Center. In 1973, the "Cape Kennedy" name reverted to Cape Canaveral.

JOHN *H. Glenn Jr.*

John Glenn joined the United States Marine Corps in 1943 as a pilot, and flew missions in both World War II and the Korean War. In 1954, he started his career as a test pilot and in 1959 became one of the seven original Mercury astronauts. Glenn served as the backup pilot for the first two Mercury flights. He became the first U.S. astronaut to orbit Earth in 1962, making three orbits before splashing down in the Atlantic Ocean. Glenn traveled into space 36 years later in October 1998 aboard the Space Shuttle *Discovery*, when he became the oldest person to fly in space.

Images (left and below) document the retrieval of a Mercury astronaut and capsule by a U.S. aircraft carrier.

Falling apart?

The equipment failure in Glenn's *Friendship 7* capsule proved typical of the entire Mercury project. In fact, NASA considered it fortunate that *Mercury 9* astronaut Gordon Cooper splashed down safely in the Pacific Ocean. By mission's end, Cooper's capsule, *Faith 7*, lost its electrical power, guidance systems, and instruments. The massive malfunctions aboard *Mercury 9* resulted in NASA's cancellation of the *Mercury 10* flight — a week-long mission in which the United States planned to set a time-spent-in-space endurance record. After Cooper's flight, NASA scrapped the Mercury Project altogether, freeing up funds and workers for its next space program — Project Gemini.

> "It was quite a day. I don't know what you can say about a day when you see four beautiful sunsets."
>
> John Glenn, 1962

John Glenn first went into space at age 40 in 1962. He returned as a senior citizen in 1998 — age 77!

On May 25, 1961, U.S. President John F. Kennedy made a bold promise in a speech given before a joint session of Congress. He announced the goal of landing a person on the Moon by the end of the decade. Kennedy's challenging statement raised the space-race competition between the United States and the Soviet Union to a new level.

An astronaut prepares to work on a satellite in the space shuttle's cargo bay.

Voskhod

Once again, the Soviet space program soared ahead of its U.S. rival. *Voskhod 1* became the first spacecraft to carry more than one person when it blasted into space on October 12, 1964, with three cosmonauts aboard. They were also the first Soviets to stay inside their spacecraft while landing. The mission itself was hastily prepared in an effort to beat the United States's Gemini project. Therefore, *Voskhod 1*'s crew had no space suits, no ejection seats and no escape tower. Nevertheless, the impact of this mission was just as great as the earlier *Sputnik 1* and *Vostok* missions. As one NASA official commented, it was "a clear indication that the Russians are continuing a large space program for the achievement of national power and prestige."

SPACE *walking*

Cosmonaut Aleksei Leonov performed the first space walk during the *Voskhod 2* mission. He spent ten minutes outside the spacecraft before reentering via an inflatable air lock. While outside the capsule, his space suit inflated so much that he could not crawl back inside. Leonov bled some air out of the suit before he could fit through the air lock. Astronauts now regularly perform space walks to repair satellites and to construct the *International Space Station* (ISS). U.S. astronauts Jim Voss and Susan Helms hold the record for the longest space walk. On March 11, 2001, they spent eight hours and fifty-six minutes outside the *International Space Station*.

Gemini

NASA's two-manned space capsule, Gemini, ultimately overtook the achievements of the Voskhod crews. The first Gemini mission to carry a crew, *Gemini 3*, blasted off on March 23, 1965. During the *Gemini 4* mission, launched on June 3, 1965, astronaut Edward White

SOYUZ

Designed as part of the Soviet Union's proposed Moon mission, the Soyuz capsule is the longest-serving manned spacecraft in the world. The program started disastrously, however. *Soyuz 1*, containing cosmonaut Vladimir Komarov, blasted off on April 23, 1967 with the intention of meeting and docking with *Soyuz 2*. Problems with *Soyuz 1* led to the cancellation of the *Soyuz 2* launch. When the *Soyuz 1* capsule reentered the atmosphere, its parachutes became entangled and the capsule crashed to the ground, killing Komarov. Since then, the Soyuz missions have had more success. The Soyuz spacecraft was eventually developed as a multi-cosmonaut vehicle for docking with and servicing space stations. Soyuz spacecraft traveled to the *Salyut* and *Mir* stations over the past thirty years and is currently being used for carrying supplies and personnel to and from the *International Space Station*.

> *"I believe that this nation should commit itself to achieving the goal, before this decade is out, of landing a man on the Moon and returning him safely to the Earth."*
>
> John F. Kennedy, addressing a special joint session of Congress, May 25, 1961

...came the first American to walk ...space. The mission also spent four days ...orbit, matching the space endurance record. ...en, *Gemini 5* spent eight days in orbit, in ...eparation for a flight to the Moon. ...mini 5 also surpassed the Soviet's ...ace endurance record for the ...st time. The following twelve ...mini missions set more ...cords. These included pushing ...e endurance record to ...urteen days, achieving ...e first automatic

reentry into the atmosphere, and several successful docking procedures with target vehicles.

Soyuz was also used for the Apollo-Soyuz Test Project, (ASTP), a historic U.S.-Soviet joint mission. The Soyuz capsule docked with an Apollo capsule in 1975. Three U.S. astronauts and two cosmonauts visited each others' spacecraft.

Transfers in space

For the first time, the Soviet Union space program found itself lagging behind the United States. After the problems with the early Soyuz flights, Soviet scientists waited nearly two years to achieve the goals outlined for the *Soyuz 1* mission: the docking of two vehicles in space and the transfer of crew from one craft to another. *Soyuz 4* and *Soyuz 5* finally achieved these goals in January 1969. By then, however, the United States led the race to land on the Moon.

Moon Race

With the successful completion of the Gemini missions, NASA turned its full attention to the Apollo program and a manned mission to the Moon. Despite extensive tests on the Apollo capsule, however, the program started with a disaster. On January 27, 1967, all three astronauts inside the *Apollo 1* capsule died in a fire during a test. NASA did not risk another crew aboard an Apollo capsule until October 11, 1968, when it launched *Apollo 7*. After that

mission, the pace increased. Two months later, *Apollo 8* became the first spacecraft to carry astronauts around the Moon. During *Apollo 8's* ten lunar orbits, the astronauts made numerous landmark sitings and took photographs. Crew members then fired rocket motors that pushed *Apollo 8* out of lunar orbit and back to Earth.

Dress rehearsals

On March 3, 1969, *Apollo 9* blasted off. The spacecraft consisted of three modules. The command module contained the astronauts during blastoff and reentry. The service module carried the power and oxygen supplies for the flight. NASA's engineers developed the lunar module to carry the astronauts down to the Moon's surface and back to the command module. *Apollo 9's* Earth-orbiting mission tested the ability of the command and service modules to disengage, turn around, and dock with the lunar module. Its astronauts conducted tests in the lunar module before returning to the command module. The final rehearsal for the Moon landing began on May 18, 1969. *Apollo 10* blasted off and left Earth's gravity to orbit the Moon. While in lunar orbit, the lunar module descended to about 9 miles (14.5 km) above the Moon's surface. Then it ascended, docked with *Apollo 10's* command and service modules and headed home. Astronauts Thomas P. Stafford, John W. Young, and Eugene A. Cernan returned safely and splashed down in the Pacific Ocean.

Astronauts Gus Grissom, Ed White, and Roger Chaffee died in a flashover during testing of the Apollo 1 *command module on January 27, 1967.*

APOLLO *emergencies*

Despite the success of later Apollo missions, the program could not have had a worse start. In 1967, a fire during a test of *Apollo 1*'s command module caused the deaths of three astronauts inside. Three years later, an explosion in *Apollo 13*'s service module while en route to the Moon led to a Deep-Space abort and cancellation of the Moon landing. The *Apollo 13* astronauts returned to Earth unharmed.

Moon landing

The first mission to land humans on the Moon launched from the Kennedy Space Center on July 16, 1969 with astronauts Neil Armstrong, Edwin "Buzz" Aldrin, and Michael Collins on board. Armstrong and Aldrin landed the lunar module on the Moon's surface on July 20, 1969. About six hours later, Armstrong became the first person to walk on the Moon, uttering the now-famous words "One small step for man, one giant leap for mankind." After a total of 21 hours 36 minutes on the Moon's surface, the lunar module blasted off to dock with the command and service modules before leaving lunar orbit and returning to Earth.

Further landings

After the success of *Apollo 11*, NASA released plans for nine more Moon landings. Only another five missions actually made it to the surface of the Moon, ending with *Apollo 17* in December 1972. During these missions, the Apollo astronauts collected samples of Moon rock for analysis back on Earth, carried out several experiments on the lunar surface, explored areas of the Moon's surface on a lunar rover vehicle, and even managed to play golf. *Apollo 14* astronaut Alan Shepard holds the record for the longest golf shot ever! NASA canceled further Moon missions after *Apollo 17* because of government funding cuts. The Soviets never landed anyone on the lunar surface. And no person has walked on the Moon in more than thirty years.

All the successful lunar landing teams brought Moon rocks, such as this one from the Apollo 17 mission, back to Earth.

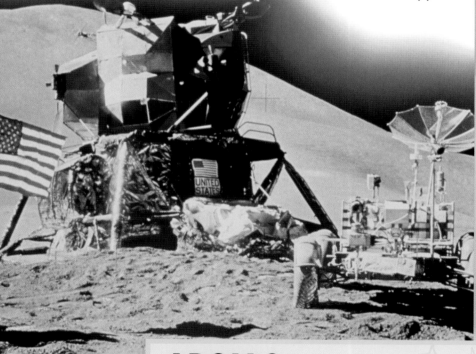

The Moon's lack of an atmosphere, and therefore no wind or rain, means that footprints left on the Moon by the Apollo astronauts will remain undisturbed for millions of years.

APOLLO *roster*

Twelve astronauts walked on the Moon. 1969: Neil Armstrong and Edwin "Buzz" Aldrin (*Apollo 11*); Allan Bean and Pete Conrad Jr. (*Apollo 12*); 1971: Edgar Mitchell and Alan Shepard (*Apollo 14*); James Irwin and David Scott (*Apollo 15*); 1972: Charles Duke Jr. and John W. Young (*Apollo 16*); Harrison Schmitt and Eugene Cernan (*Apollo 17*).

SPACE *lifeboat*

One of the problems of having a crew in space for long periods of time is how to rescue them in case of an emergency. There might not be time to launch a rescue mission, so space station designers used the concept of a "lifeboat" capsule. The Soviets set up a space station emergency plan that used the same capsule in which the cosmonauts arrived. Alternative "space lifeboats" under consideration for the *ISS* include small space planes, such as the X-33, X-38, and the *HL-20*, which could break away from the *ISS*, reenter the atmosphere and glide down to a landing strip. Budget constraints shelved many of these ideas. The *ISS* continues to use a Soyuz capsule to transport the crew and supplies to and from Earth. A Soyuz *TMA-1* emergency spacecraft returned the *ISS* crew to Earth in May 2003 after the disintegration of the Space Shuttle *Columbia* on February 1, 2003.

During the late 1990s, several Space Shuttle missions visited and docked with the Soviet Space Station Mir.

Salyut

After the Moon landings, scientists focused on establishing a space station. The Soviets took the lead once again by launching the space station *Salyut* on April 19, 1971. But success turned to disaster. The first crew, who stayed on *Salyut 1* for twenty-three days, died when their *Soyuz 11* capsule depressurized during reentry. Other setbacks for the Salyut program included the losses of *Salyut 2* and *Salyut 3*. The last two Salyut stations, *Salyut* and *Salyut 7*, however, proved very successful. *Salyut 6*, launched in 1977, was inhabited for a total of 676 days, with individual stays lasting up to 185 days. *Salyut 7* was launched in 1982. Twenty-four different cosmonauts (including cosmonauts from France and India) visited and inhabited the station for a total 861 days, recording durations of up to 236 days in space. The Soviets planned to bring *Salyut 7* back to Earth on the Space Shuttle *Buran*. Instead, the Soviets canceled the program. *Salyut 7* burned during reentry in a fiery show on February 7, 1991.

Skylab

The U.S. space station program relied heavily on technology used for the Apollo Moon missions. NASA engineers constructed *Skylab* using spare Saturn V rockets available after the cancellation of the lunar missions. Problems with *Skylab* arose soon after its launch on May 14, 1973. The solar shield designed to protect *Skylab* from the Sun ripped off during ascent, which caused the internal temperature to soar to 126 degrees Fahrenheit (52 degrees Centigrade). Successive missions to *Skylab* repaired the problem by installing a sunshade. The third Space Shuttle flight to visit *Skylab* was supposed to boost it into a higher, safer orbit. However, delays in the Space Shuttle program and an unexpected deterioration in *Skylab*'s orbit led to its spectacular, fiery reentry over Australia on July 11, 1979.

Mir *Space Station*

Mir was the last effort of the Soviet space program. Initially designed to last for five years, it stayed in orbit for a further ten years. *Mir* survived the collapse of the Soviet Union, but it required the financial assistance of the United States to keep it aloft, a sign of how far behind the Soviet space program had fallen compared to its U.S. counterpart. Throughout its operational lifetime, problems beset *Mir*, including a collision with another spacecraft, which, miraculously, did little serious damage. The Soviets abandoned several of the modules designed to attach to *Mir* because of a lack of funds. In fact, only an annual gift of $100 million dollars from NASA helped keep *Mir* in orbit. This money paid for a "guest astronaut" on board *Mir*, as well as a total of nine visits by the Space Shuttle to the ailing station.

"You're in charge, but don't touch the controls."

Soviet cosmonauts to U.S. Astronaut Shannon Lucid when they left her on Mir to go on their space walk.

NASA astronauts pose inside Skylab prior to its launch into orbit.

LIVING *in space*

Astronauts living in space do many of the same things that they would do on Earth. However, some of these things are done a little differently. Food can float away when it is eaten in space, so sticky foods work best on missions and no crumbly foods are taken. Some astronauts prefer foods with strong flavors. The lack of gravity aboard the *ISS* causes blood to flow more easily to the head, giving an astronaut a feeling of blocked sinuses, diminishing his or her ability to taste milder foods. Going to the bathroom is another tricky problem. To combat this, the space toilets use a sort of vacuum that carries waste away from the astronaut's body. Finally, getting enough exercise is one of the most important things to do when living in zero gravity for long periods of time. Without gravity to work against, the body's muscles and bones tend to waste away. Exercise maintains muscle tone and body strength, which helps the astronauts avoid problems when readjusting to Earth's gravity.

Open doors on the Space Shuttle's cargo bay reveal the robotic arm used to launch and retrieve satellites.

In the end, the effort to keep *Mir* in orbit became too much. On March 23, 2001, *Mir* "deorbited," entered Earth's atmosphere, and burned up over the Pacific Ocean.

SHUTTLE *disasters*

On January 28, 1986, the failure of the seals on one of the booster rockets led to an explosion that destroyed the space Shuttle *Challenger* and killed all seven astronauts on board. Tragically, on February 1, 2003, the Space Shuttle *Columbia* burned up during reentry into the atmosphere, again killing all seven crew members. One theory about the possible cause points to pieces of insulating foam that fell off the fuel tank during *Columbia*'s launch. NASA engineers believe that the impact of the foam pieces damaged heat-shield tiles on the left wing, resulting in the spacecraft's destruction.

Space Shuttle

The next stage in space exploration was the development of a reusable space launcher. Such technology would allow the building of larger space stations while in orbit, as well as the creation of enormous rockets for interplanetary journeys and manned Mars expeditions. However, NASA's forced budgetary restrictions throughout the 1970s led to the cancellation of many of these projects, with only the Space Shuttle surviving. Despite the fact that no shuttles were launched until 1981, NASA remained an enormous organization after the lunar missions, which elevated costs. Even the shuttle project itself faced drastic cuts, with the planned fleet size reduced and the initial launch delayed by three years — which also resulted in the loss of *Skylab* in 1979 (see page 37). In practice, the Space Shuttle has also failed to fulfill many of its original goals, especially the idea that it could provide cheap rocket vehicles for other uses. The comparative expense of the Space Shuttle, combined with the disastrous failure of two missions, led several of NASA's customers (most noticeably the U.S. Air Force), to return to conventional rocket launchers for missile tests or to put communication or other satellites in orbit.

Not all bad news

However, the Shuttle's successes include keeping NASA's manned space program on track. Each launch can carry seven astronauts who, after placing the satellite cargo into orbit, often perform other experiments and research. This feature allows NASA to highlight the advantages of putting people in space as well as robots. One shining example of this was the successful mission to repair the Hubble Space Telescope (HST) in 1993. Space Shuttle astronauts replaced several faulty parts and corrected the HST's "sight." Without this repair, the multi-million dollar orbiting telescope was relatively useless.

Into the future

The Space Shuttle also proved vital in the construction of the massive *International Space Station*. Its large payload bay can carry many of the *ISS* modules into orbit, and the crew on board can perform space walks — also called extra vehicular activities (EVA) — to fix the modules into place. Despite the recent, tragic destruction of the space shuttle *Columbia*, the space shuttle program will continue to fly. NASA remains confident that the existing fleet of shuttles will operate until 2015.

The Soviet space shuttle Buran *stands on the launchpad attached to a mighty Energia rocket.*

Soviet *shuttle*

Eager to build their own reusable spacecraft, the Soviets considered many designs before they opted for something that was, essentially, a direct copy of the U.S. Space Shuttle. The project took about twelve years to develop. The Soviet shuttle, *Buran* ("Snowstorm" in Russian), blasted into space on its first mission on November 15, 1988. An Energia rocket — the most powerful rocket launcher ever built — launched the flawless mission. It carried no cosmonauts and the entire flight was automatically controlled. *Buran* separated from the launcher, entered orbit, then fired its retrorockets and reentered the atmosphere, gliding to a landing at 162 mph (260 kph). Unfortunately, it was *Buran*'s one — and only — flight. Funds dried up, and the Soviet Moon project was officially cancelled in 1993, when it disappeared completely from the Soviet government's official budgets.

FUTURE SPACE MISSIONS

The future holds many challenge for the human exploration of space. Following the second shuttle disaster, the very question of whether humans should travel into space is in doubt, especially in the face of some startling robot probe successes. But human space exploration seems certain, with some spectacular projects on the horizon.

When completed, the International Space Station will be the largest man-made object orbiting Earth. An artist's rendering shows what the ISS will look like when completed.

International cooperation

With the end of the space race came a period of unprecedented cooperation between the Soviets and the United States. A number of joint missions, such as the first Space Shuttle docking with the *Mir* Space Station in late 1995, occurred. This level of cooperation extended even further

beginning in 1998 with the building of the *International Space Station (ISS)*. The enormous orbiting space platform is currently under construction with the cooperation of the United States, Russia and other European countries, Canada, and Japan. It will take more than forty flights to complete all phases of the *ISS*.

FLIGHT *from orbit*

One of the potential advantages of a permanent manned space station is that it presents an excellent starting point for space missions. Current rockets use the majority of their fuel to escape Earth's gravitational pull. Tremendous amounts of fuel could be saved by starting from a point in space, making spaceflight far more economical.

...e finished station will be more ...n 360 feet (110 m) wide. ...e *ISS* has been visible in the ...ht sky since it was first ...nched in 1998.

...ission to Mars

...ns are underway for humans ...travel to Mars, one of our ...rest neighbors in the Solar ...tem. A trip to Mars will take ...ut nine months one way. Once there, astronauts ...uld need to spend time on the Red Planet's ...face waiting for Earth and Mars to align correctly ...fore beginning the return trip. Two NASA robot ...bes are scheduled to visit Mars in early 2004. ...other Mars mission is set for 2007, with a ...nned mission to follow in the next few decades.

The idea of life on Mars and other planets sparks imaginations.

...aster rockets

...nventional rockets that explore the immediate region of space are expensive and relatively inefficient. A new form of propulsion is necessary to explore Deep-Space. Proposals for new types of rocket power include using lasers to push spacecraft along and using solar particles for propulsion energy. Another possibility actually in use is an ion propulsion system. Charged particles (ions) are created by stripping xenon atoms of their electrons. The particles accelerate to produce a jet of gas. As gas shoots out the back of the ion motor — at a top speed of 68,000 mph (109,430 kph) — it propels the spacecraft forward. The first U.S. spacecraft to use such technology as its primary fuel was *Deep Space 1*, launched in 1998. Ion-propulsion powered spacecraft are very fuel-efficient and can potentially reach speeds — although it takes a lot longer to do so — well in excess of what conventional rockets achieve. Ion propulsion steadily increases its thrust by 15 to 20 mph (25 to 32 kph). Tests in 1998 revealed that an ion-propulsion vehicle could attain a final cruising speed of 33,000 mph (53,100 kph).

> *"And then, the Earth being small, mankind will migrate into space, and will cross the airless Saharas which separate planet from planet and sun from sun."*
>
> Winwood Reade
> The Martyrdom of Man, 1872

> *"The Earth is a cradle of the mind, but we cannot live forever in a cradle."*
>
> Konstantin E. Tsiolkovsky, 1896

One of the Viking probes that landed on Mars in 1976 sent back this view of the Martian surface.

THE RED *planet*

One of the proposed Mars missions includes producing fuel and oxygen supplies on the planet itself once astronauts land there. In theory, a robot factory could harvest carbon dioxide from the Martian atmosphere and water from the frozen poles. It could then turn these into methane and oxygen to power a rocket for a return trip to Earth.

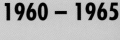

1500 – 1929

• Circa 1500s: Chinese official Wan-Hu affixes forty-seven rockets to a chair in an attempt at rocket-powered flight. The rockets, chair, and Wan-Hu all vanish in the explosion.

• War of 1812: British forces use Congreve rockets against Fort McHenry. The rocket attack inspires Francis Scott Key to write the words to the U.S. national anthem.

• March 1926: Robert Goddard launches the world's first liquid-fueled rocket. It shoots up about 41 feet (12.5 m), travels a distance of 183 feet (56 m), and reaches a speed of 60 mph (96.5 kph) during its 2.5-second flight.

1930 – 1949

• 1930s: The Germans move Wernher von Braun and his team of scientists and technicians to a secret base at Peenemünde to work on the V2 rocket.

• August 1943: An Allied air raid destroys the base at Peenemünde. The Germans move von Braun and his team to another secret base at Nordhausen.

• 1944: The Germans launch V2 rockets at Allied targets. In the last year of WWII, nearly 4,300 V2 rockets rain down on Antwerp, Belgium, and on London and Paris.

• 1945: WWII ends in Europe. Wernher von Braun and many team members surrender to Allied troops. They continue their rocket research in the United States. Other scientists go to the Soviet Union.

1950 – 1959

• October 1957: The Soviet Union launches Sputnik 1, the world's first artificial satellite. It emits a simple radio signal for three weeks and remains in orbit until early 1958, when it burns up in the atmosphere.

• November 1957: Within a month of launching Sputnik 1, the Soviets launch Sputnik 2. The spacecraft carries the first living being to travel into space — a dog named Laika. She dies aboard the spacecraft.

• January 1958: The U.S. launches its first space probe, Explorer 1. Instruments aboard the spacecraft discover the Van Allen Radiation Belts, a region of high radiation encircling Earth at the equator.

1960 – 1965

• April 1961: Soviet Yuri Gagarin becomes the first per to travel into space. His Vosto mission lasts only 108 minute He completes one Earth orbit.

• May 1961: Alan B. Shepard becomes the first U.S. astron in space. Freedom 7, his Mer capsule, reaches an altitude of 116 miles (186 km).

• February 1962: John H. Glen becomes the first U.S. astrono to orbit Earth. His Mercury capsule, Friendship 7, spends 4 hours 55 minutes in flight, including several orbits of Ear

• June 1963: Valentina Teresh becomes the first woman to tra in space aboard Vostok 6.

66 – 1969

• anuary 1967: A fire on board o 1 kills three astronauts e launchpad during a test.

• tober 1968: First manned t of the Apollo capsules a three astronauts aboard o 7 orbit Earth 163 times.

• cember 1968: Apollo 8 mes the first Apollo mission ched by a Saturn V rocket. he first manned mission bit the Moon

• y 1969: Apollo 10 travels e Moon and releases the module, which descends out 9 miles (14.5 km) e the lunar surface.

• y 1969: Neil Armstrong Buzz Aldrin become the men to walk on the Moon g the Apollo 11 mission.

1970 – 1979

• April 1971: The Soviet Union launches the world's first manned space station, Salyut 1. The station orbits Earth for 175 days, then burns up upon reentry into Earth's atmosphere.

• May 1973: The U.S. launches its first space station, Skylab, into orbit. Problems during liftoff cause an improper deployment of a heat shield. Skylab is uninhabitable until repairs are performed during the next mission.

1980 – 1989

• April 1981: The Space Shuttle Columbia becomes the world's first reusable spacecraft. Astronauts Robert Crippen and John W. Young orbit for two days before landing at Edwards Air Force Base in California.

• January 1986: Space Shuttle Challenger explodes seventy-three seconds after takeoff, killing all seven astronauts on board. Engineers point to a faulty seal in one of the rocket boosters as the cause of the explosion. As a result, the U.S. grounds its manned space fleet.

• February 1986: Soviets launch the core module of the Space Station Mir. The space station orbits Earth for the next fifteen years, with further modules added. Mir reenters the atmosphere and burns up in March 2001.

• September 1988: The U.S. manned space program resumes with the launch of the Space Shuttle Discovery. Five astronauts successfully complete a four-day mission.

1990 – 2003

• April 1990: The Space Shuttle Discovery places the Hubble Space Telescope (HST) into orbit.

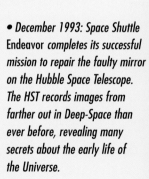

• December 1993: Space Shuttle Endeavor completes its successful mission to repair the faulty mirror on the Hubble Space Telescope. The HST records images from farther out in Deep-Space than ever before, revealing many secrets about the early life of the Universe.

• November 1998: The first module of the International Space Station is launched from the Baikonur Cosmodrome at Tyuratam and put into orbit. One month later, the second module is attached. Before long, the ISS becomes the largest object to ever orbit Earth.

• February 2003: The space shuttle Columbia disintegrates during reentry, killing all seven crew members. NASA cancels all manned space missions for at least one year.

altitude the height above Earth's surface. Space starts at an altitude of about 100 miles (160 km) above Earth.

apogee the greatest distance a satellite or other spacecraft travels in its orbit from the center of its planet of origin. (*See also* perigee.)

astronaut the name used by Western countries to describe a person who travels into space. It comes from the Greek *astron*, meaning star, and *nautes*, meaning sailor. (*See also* cosmonaut.)

atmosphere the thin, gassy layer that surrounds many planets. A planet's atmosphere thins out farther from the planet's surface, eventually dwindling into nothing.

boosters powerful rockets that form part of the first stage of a multi-stage launch vehicle. The Space Shuttle's reusable booster rockets contain solid fuel. After they burn out, the boosters parachute to the surface, where they are retrieved and reused on future Space Shuttle missions.

Congreve rockets artillery rockets devised by Englishman William Congreve in 1804. A long stick, about 16.5 feet (5 m) long, steadied the rockets in flight.

cosmonaut Russian for a person who travels into space. It derives from the Greek *kosmos*, meaning the Universe, and *nautes*, meaning sailor. (*See also* astronaut.)

electron a negatively charged particle found in all atoms.

eject to remove, often forcibly — especially when a pilot escapes from an aircraft while strapped to his or her seat. Once clear of the aircraft, the pilot parachutes safely to the ground.

FAI: (La Fédération Aéronautique Internationale (International Aeronautical Federation) the French organization that oversees all aspects of air sports around the world, including space records.

heat shield a protective layer designed to protect the spacecraft and its occupants from the searing heat experienced during reentry.

ion propulsion a type of rocket power that uses charged atoms to accelerate a craft.

International Space Station (ISS) a space station under construction through the joint efforts of the United States, Russia, Canada, and Japan. When completed, the *ISS* will be the largest object ever assembled in orbit. It is visible to the naked eye in the night sky.

liftoff the moment when a rocket starts its ascent by lifting clear of the launchpad. NASA's Space Shuttle fires its rockets on the count of seven and proceeds to liftoff on zero. European missions fire their rockets on zero and do not start liftoff for another seven seconds.

liquid fuel fuel that is used in a liquid form. Liquid-fuel rockets use a fuel and an oxidizer that are kept so cold they liquify. The liquids are then mixed and ignited to produce a blast of hot gases that push the spacecraft forward. They provide a spacecraft's pilots with a greater degree of control than solid-fuel rockets, which cannot be switched off once ignited.

maket the Russian word for "dummy." *Maket* was printed on mannequins launched during tests of space-capsule ejection seats so that people who found the full-size dummies would not panic and attempt rescue efforts or be frightened, thinking they found a "visitor" from outer space.

module a portion of a spacecraft. For example, the *Apollo 11* spacecraft consisted of three modules. These were the service module containing the fuel, oxygen, and supplies for the mission; the command module for traveling to the Moon and returning to Earth; and the lunar module for landing on the Moon's surface.

National Aeronautics and Space Administration (NASA) the U.S. space agency established in 1958 to coordinate all types of U.S. space missions.

it the usually elliptical (egg-shaped) path of an object, such satellite or a moon, around a larger body, such as a planet.

igee the orbital point at which a satellite or other spacecraft travels est to the center of its planet of origin. (*See also* apogee.)

totype the first form or model of something, such as a rocket.

itburo the supreme policy-making governmental organization he Communist Party and the Soviet Union.

ntry the return of a spacecraft into Earth's atmosphere.

ket a vehicle that uses a jet of gases to push it forward. ventional rockets use a mixture of fuels and oxidizers that ignite roduce a jet of expanding hot gases that create thrust.

ssian a citizen of Russia, or of the former Soviet Union.

ellite an object, such as a spacecraft or a moon, that ts a larger celestial body, such as a planet.

id fuel fuel used in solid form. Solid-fuel rockets contain the fuel oxidizer already mixed together, usually in a granular form. Solid s are easy to handle and produce a great deal of thrust. However, do not offer much control and cannot be switched off once ignited.

:e Shuttle a series of reusable spacecraft developed by NASA started operational flights in 1981. All parts of the Space Shuttle em are reusable, except for the giant orange fuel tank that burns up e atmosphere after it is released. The rocket boosters parachute back arth as soon as their fuel is spent and are recovered shortly after takeoff. e end of each mission, the shuttle itself glides to a landing at an airstrip ther California or Florida.

ace station a large, manned, artificial satellite designed end a long period of time in space in order to provide a base for ntific, medical, and military research. It may also offer docking ports other spacecraft as well as launching facilities for future space missions.

space suit a special suit worn by astronauts and cosmonauts to protect from the harsh environment of space outside of a spacecraft. Sealed and pressurized, a space suit provides its wearer with breathing air, temperature control, communications links, and protection from high levels of radiation.

space walk; extravehicular activity (EVA) the part of a space mission during which an astronaut or cosmonaut leaves the spacecraft to perform various functions, such as repairing a satellite, transferring to another spacecraft, or building a module.

splashdown the controlled landing of a spacecraft in water at the end of a space mission. Up until the advent of the Space Shuttle, all manned NASA missions splashed down in the ocean before retrieval. In contrast, all manned Soviet space missions landed on solid ground.

stratosphere a layer of the atmosphere that starts at an altitude of about 7 miles (11km) and extends up to about 31 miles (50 km).

suborbital flight a flight path by a spacecraft that does not complete an orbit of Earth.

Soviet Union (USSR, the Union of Soviet Socialist Republics) a communist nation which consisted of Russia and several other countries, including Estonia, Latvia, Georgia, Uzbekistan, Tajikistan, and the Ukraine. Established in 1917, the Soviet Union grew in size, reaching its peak between 1946 and 1991 — when it was the largest country on the planet. In 1991, the nation split into individual states with none of them under communist rule.

Zenit the group name for the very early Soviet spy satellites capable of taking images of Earth from orbit. The Soviet could control the positioning of these satellites. *Zenit 2* and *Zenit 4* were part of the Vostok program.

FURTHER INFORMATION

Books

Failure Is Not an Option: Mission Control from Mercury to Apollo 13 and Beyond. Gene Kranz (Thorndike Paperback Bestsellers)

Flight: My Life in Mission Control. Chris Kraft (Penguin Putnam)

The Rocket Men: Vostok and Voskhod, the First Soviet Manned Spaceflights. Rex Hall and David J. Shayler (Springer-Verlag)

Sputnik: The Shock of the Century. Paul Dickson (Walker)

Star-Crossed Orbits: Inside the U.S. – Russian Space Alliance. James Oberg (McGraw-Hill)

Web Sites

www.bbc.co.uk/dna/h2g2/alabaater/A862689
Discover the details and the secrecy behind the world's first manned spaceflight.

www.cnn.com/SPECIALS/space/glenn/news/where.now
Meet the seven men of the Mercury Project.

www.encounter2001.com/events/poa3.htm
Read how animals paved the way for human spaceflight in this history of animal astronauts.

www.nasm.si.edu/apollo/AS11/
Learn all about *Apollo 11* through a series of links and images.

quest.arc.nasa.gov/space/teachers/rocket/history.html
Explore the origins of rocket science.